THE
COUPLES
BUCKET LIST
BOOK

Golden Lion Publications

Golden Lion Publications © Copyright 2021 - All rights reserved.
The content contained within this book may not be reproduced, duplicated or transmitted without direct written permission from the author or the publisher.

Under no circumstances will any blame or legal responsibility be held against the publisher, or author, for any damages, reparation, or monetary loss due to the information contained within this book, either directly or indirectly.

Legal Notice:
This book is copyright protected. It is only for personal use. You cannot amend, distribute, sell, use, quote or paraphrase any part, or the content within this book, without the consent of the author or publisher.

Disclaimer Notice:
Please note the information contained within this document is for educational and entertainment purposes only. All effort has been executed to present accurate, up to date, reliable, complete information. No warranties of any kind are declared or implied. Readers acknowledge that the author is not engaged in the rendering of legal, financial, medical or professional advice. The content within this book has been derived from various sources. Please consult a licensed professional before attempting any techniques outlined in this book.

By reading this document, the reader agrees that under no circumstances is the author responsible for any losses, direct or indirect, that are incurred as a result of the use of the information contained within this document, including, but not limited to, errors, omissions, or inaccuracies.

ISBN: 9798794615708

WIN $300*

YOU AND YOUR PARTNER HAVE THE CHANCE TO WIN $300.

FLIP TO THE END OF THE BOOK TO FIND OUT HOW TO ENTER OUR EXCLUSIVE COMPETITION.

*OFFER ENDS MAY 1ST 2022.

CONTENTS

INDOOR DATES ♥ 9

OUTDOOR DATES ♥ 33

ACTIVITY DATES ♥ 55

FOOD & DRINK DATES ♥ 81

OTHER DATES ♥ 89

SEASONAL DATES ♥ 105

INDOOR DATES

These are fun, creative activities you can do with your partner to spend quality time with each other without having to leave the house. Best of all...Most of them are free!

001

DO EACH OTHER'S MAKEUP AND TAKE A PICTURE OF THE END RESULT.

Insert Picture Here

002

TRY A NO–EQUIPMENT WORKOUT EXERCISE WITH YOUR PARTNER. YOU CAN FIND SOME PROGRAMS ON YOUTUBE.

Insert Picture Here

003

PAINT EACH OTHER. YOU CAN GRAB A CANVAS OR JUST A PIECE OF PAPER WITH WATERCOLORS.

004

MAKE A DIY KITE. YOU CAN FIND COUNTLESS TUTORIALS ON YOUTUBE. EXTRA POINTS IF IT CAN FLY.

005

GET SOME MODELLING CLAY AND TRY TO SCULPT EACH OTHER.

Insert Picture Here

006

DO THE PICNIC TABLE CHALLENGE. IT MIGHT SEEM HARD AT FIRST BUT TRUST ME IT'S COMPLETELY ACHIEVABLE.

007

MAKE A SOAP. YOU CAN FIND KITS ON AMAZON AND INSTRUCTIONS ON HOW TO MAKE IT ON YOUTUBE.

008

MAKE A MOVIE. YOU CAN WRITE THE DIALOGUE, CREATE COSTUMES AND SHOOT IT ON YOUR PHONE. LET YOUR CREATIVITY FLOW.

Insert Picture Here

009

MAKE ORIGAMI TOGETHER. YOU CAN ORDER ORIGAMI PAPER ONLINE OR USE PAPER YOU HAVE AT HOME.

Insert Picture Here

010

PLAY VIDEO GAMES. THIS CAN BE ANYTHING FROM MARIO KART TO FREE ONLINE GAMES. MAKE SURE YOU HAVE A BET PLACED FOR EXTRA ACTION.

Insert Picture Here

011

WATCH A TERRIBLE MOVIE. NOTHING BONDS LIKE A BAD SPOOF FILM! TRY TO FIND ONE WITH A REALLY LOW RATING. THE WORSE THE BETTER.

Insert Picture Here

012

PLAY A BOARD GAME. HEADS UP COUNTS TOO.

013

SET UP BEER PONG AND SEE WHO IS THE CHAMPION. YOU CAN INVITE FRIENDS OVER AS WELL.

Insert Picture Here

014

PLAY TWISTER. WE ALL KNOW HOW THIS IS GOING TO END.

Insert Picture Here

015

SOLVE A PUZZLE. A GREAT WAY TO CREATE A STRONGER BOND WITH YOUR PARTNER BY TALKING AND HELPING EACH OTHER OUT.

016

TRY YOGA TOGETHER. YOU CAN FOLLOW A TUTORIAL ON YOUTUBE. HOWEVER, IT DOESN'T HAVE TO BE "TRADITIONAL YOGA".

Insert Picture Here

017

TRY TO RECREATE LIFE HACKS FROM YOUTUBE. SOME OF THEM ARE RIDICULOUS BUT MIGHT ACTUALLY WORK.

Insert Picture Here

018

WATCH EXPERIMENT VIDEOS YOU CAN DO AT HOME TOGETHER ON YOUTUBE AND TRY THEM OUT.

019

REVISIT YOUR CHILDHOOD PHOTOS. IF YOU DON'T HAVE A PHOTO ALBUM I'M SURE YOU CAN FIND SOME GOOD PICTURES ON FACEBOOK.

020

CREATE A BATH BOMB FROM SCRATCH THEN USE IT TOGETHER.

021

CREATE AND LAUNCH YOUR OWN ROCKET. YOU CAN FIND TUTORIALS ON YOUTUBE.

Insert Picture Here

022

CREATE YOUR OWN CUSTOM T-SHIRTS. YOU CAN EITHER SEND IT TO A COMPANY TO PRINT OR DO IT YOURSELVES FROM HOME.

Insert Picture Here

023

LEARN A DANCE CHOREOGRAPHY TOGETHER FROM ANY SONG.

OUTDOOR DATES

These dates require you to leave you're house. They will help you bring you closer together with your spouse while sharing experiences you will remember for a lifetime.

024

CREATE SIDEWALK CHALK ART. YOU WILL ALWAYS HAVE A PIECE OF ART REPRESENTING YOUR RELATIONSHIP ON A SIDEWALK.

Insert Picture Here

025

GO TO A YARD SALE AND SEE WHAT COOL THINGS YOU CAN FIND.

Insert Picture Here

026

GO ROLLER–SKATING. THIS IS A GREAT WAY TO GET YOUR BLOOD PUMPING AND SHARE AN ADRENALINE RUSH TOGETHER.

Insert Picture Here

027

GO THROUGH A CORN MAZE TOGETHER. THIS IS A GREAT WAY TO SEE HOW WELL YOU TWO CAN SOLVE A PROBLEM TOGETHER.

Insert Picture Here

028

GO TO AN AQUARIUM. THERE IS SOMETHING CALMING ABOUT WATCHING FISH SWIM.

Insert Picture Here

029

GO TO A ZOO. IT'S A GREAT PLACE TO EXPERIENCE NATURE WITH YOUR SPOUSE.

Insert Picture Here

030

GO TO AN ART GALLERY. THIS IS A GREAT FREE DATE WHICH USUALLY CONSISTS OF FREE SNACKS AND WINE.

Insert Picture Here

031

GO ON A MUSEUM DATE. YOU WILL GET TO SEE YOUR PARTNERS PERSPECTIVE ON CERTAIN ART PIECES.

Insert Picture Here

032

GO HORSEBACK RIDING. YOU MIGHT GET THROWN OFF THE HORSE BUT AT LEAST YOU WILL SPEND TIME TOGETHER IN THE HOSPITAL.

Insert Picture Here

033

TAKE A HOT AIR BALLOON RIDE. THERE'S NOTHING MORE ROMANTIC THAN LOOKING AT THE CITY FROM A BIRDS EYE VIEW WITH YOUR PARTNER.

Insert Picture Here

034

GO TO A BAKERY OR BREWERY TOUR. EVERY TOUR COMES WITH TASTY FREE SAMPLES.

Insert Picture Here

035

RENT A TWO SEATED BIKE AND RIDE AROUND. THIS IS BEST DONE IN A NON—CROWDED PLACE.

Insert Picture Here

036

CREATE A CAMP-FIRE AND COOK MARSHMALLOWS ON A STICK AND OTHER DELICIOUS SNACKS.

Insert Picture Here

037

GO AROUND ON A PHOTOGRAPHY SPREE AND GO OVER THE PHOTOS DURING LUNCH.

Insert Picture Here

038

GO SKIP ROCKS. YOU CAN BOTH COME TO A MUTUAL AGREEMENT ON THE WINNERS REWARD.

Insert Picture Here

039

ADD A LOVE LOCK TO A BRIDGE. IF THERE ARE NONE IN YOUR AREA, CREATE THE FIRST ONE.

Insert Picture Here

040

TAKE A GONDOLA RIDE.

Insert Picture Here

50

041

GO WATCH A PLAY. MAKE SURE YOU BOTH AGREE ON THE PLAY OR RANDOMLY PICK ONE WITHOUT KNOWING THE CONCEPT.

Insert Picture Here

042

GO TO A PLANETARIUM. THERE IS SOMETHING MAGICAL ABOUT LOOKING AT THE STARS.

Insert Picture Here

043

ATTEND A LIVE CONCERT. MAKE SURE IT'S A GENRE OR ARTIST YOU BOTH LIKE.

Insert Picture Here

044

HAVE A CASINO NIGHT. JUST MAKE SURE YOU DON'T SPEND MORE THAN YOU CAN AFFORD TO LOSE.

ACTIVITY DATES

These dates will get your blood pumping and the adrenaline rushing through your body. You are guaranteed to have a beautiful experience with your partner.

045

ATTEND A KARAOKE NIGHT AND SING A DUET. YOU MIGHT NEED SOME ALCOHOL BEFORE ATTEMPTING THIS.

Insert Picture Here

046

CRASH A PARTY. WEAR SOMETHING FANCY AND PRETEND YOU KNOW SOMEONE. YOU GET FREE DRINKS AND SNACKS, IF YOU DON'T GET CAUGHT.

Insert Picture Here

047

WATCH AN IMPROV SHOW. THESE SHOWS ARE USUALLY REALLY CHEAP AND SOMETIMES FREE.

048

TAKE A PAINTING CLASS. THEN YOU CAN COMPARE WITH EACH OTHER ON WHO THE BETTER ARTIST IS.

Insert Picture Here

049

GO TO A POTTERY CLASS. IF YOU'VE EVER SEEN THE MOVIE 'GHOST' YOU KNOW WHAT TO EXPECT.

Insert Picture Here

050

RIDE A ROLLER—COASTER TOGETHER. AS SCARY AS IT MAY SOUND IT WILL BE A MASSIVE ADRENALINE RUSH FOR BOTH OF YOU.

Insert Picture Here

051

GO ICE SKATING. THIS IS THE PERFECT ROMANTIC ACTIVITY. YOU CAN GLIDE SLOWLY AS YOU GET TO KNOW EACH OTHER BETTER.

Insert Picture Here

052

GO TO TRIVIA NIGHT AT A BAR. LET SEE WHO KNOWS MORE.

Insert Picture Here

053

GO TO AN ESCAPE ROOM. THIS IS THE PERFECT SETTING TO TEST HOW WELL YOU WORK TOGETHER. YOU CAN TRY IT WITH FRIENDS TOO.

Insert Picture Here

054

GO BOWLING. IF YOU HATE BOWLING, YOU CAN ALWAYS SET UP BEER BOTTLES AT HOME.

Insert Picture Here

055

GO SKEET SHOOTING. IT'S LIKE HUNTING BUT NO ANIMALS GET HURT.

056

GO SKYDIVING. MAKE SURE TO TAKE A PICTURE IF YOU SURVIVE.

Insert Picture Here

057

TRY OUT ROCK CLIMBING. AS LONG AS YOU HAVE GOOD UPPER BODY STRENGTH LOVE CLIMBING THIS DATE IS PERFECT.

Insert Picture Here

058

SWIM WITH DOLPHINS. THIS WILL CHANGE YOUR LIFE.

Insert Picture Here

059

HAVE AN ARCADE DATE. YOU CAN ALWAYS COMPETE FOR THE HIGHEST SCORE AND PLACE A BET FOR THE LOSER.

Insert Picture Here

060

GO ZIP LINING. THE ADRENALINE RUSH YOU WILL GET FROM THIS IS INDESCRIBABLE.

Insert Picture Here

061

TRY ARCHERY OR AXE THROWING. IT'S MUCH HARDER THAN IT SEEMS BUT IT'S GUARANTEED TO GIVE YOU A GOOD TIME.

Insert Picture Here

062

GO FOR A HELICOPTER TOUR. IF YOU'RE FEELING LIKE A DAREDEVIL YOU CAN TRY A STUNT PLANE EXPERIENCE.

Insert Picture Here

063

PLAY MINI GOLF. YOU GET THE SAME AMOUNT OF FUN FROM NORMAL GOLF WITHOUT HAVING TO DRIVE AROUND TO FIND YOUR BALLS.

Insert Picture Here

064

GO TO A FAIR. YOU WILL ALWAYS FIND SOMETHING TO DO AND MAYBE EVEN WIN SOME PRIZES.

Insert Picture Here

065

GO TO A TRAMPOLINE PARK. IF YOU WANT TO FEEL LIKE A CHILD AGAIN THIS IS THE PERFECT PLACE.

066

RUN A MARATHON TOGETHER. NOT ONLY WILL YOU BE DOING A HEALTHY ACTIVITY TOGETHER, YOU CAN ALSO DO IT FOR A GOOD CAUSE.

067

GO TO A HAUNTED HOUSE OR GHOST TOURS.

UNLESS YOU'RE TOO SCARED.

Insert Picture Here

068

GO PLAY BINGO. YOU NEVER KNOW HOW LUCKY YOU MIGHT GET.

Insert Picture Here

069

PLAY TENNIS. IF YOU CAN'T FIND A TENNIS COURT NEAR YOU, YOU CAN ALWAYS GET A PING PONG SET TO PLAY AT HOME.

FOOD & DRINK DATES

These dates will wake up your taste-buds.

070

GO WINE TASTING OR GET SOME WINE AND TRY THEM AT HOME.

Insert Picture Here

071

COOK SOMETHING TOGETHER YOU HAVE NEVER COOKED BEFORE.

Insert Picture Here

072

MAKE YOUR OWN PIZZA FROM SCRATCH. THIS INCLUDES THE DOUGH. MAKE SURE TO ADD YOUR FAVORITE TOPPINGS ON IT.

Insert Picture Here

073

CREATE A DESSERT TOGETHER WITH YOUR OWN SPIN. YOU CAN EITHER FIND A RECIPE IN A RECIPE BOOK OR LOOK UP A YOUTUBE VIDEO.

Insert Picture Here

074

GO TO A RESTAURANT THAT FEATURES A CUISINE NEITHER OF YOU HAVE TRIED. ORDER TWO DIFFERENT MEALS AND TASTE ONE ANOTHER'S.

075

CREATE COCKTAILS AT HOME. IF YOU DON'T DRINK ALCOHOL YOU CAN CREATE AN ALCOHOL FREE COCKTAIL.

Insert Picture Here

076

GO TO A CHEESE TASTING. YOU NEVER KNOW WHAT DIFFERENT FLAVOURS YOU MIGHT UNCOVER.

Insert Picture Here

OTHER DATES

This chapter is dedicated to all the weird, relaxing, funny and downright outrageous dates you can go on.

077

GO TO ZOOM THERAPY TOGETHER. EVEN IF YOU MIGHT THINK YOU DON'T NEED THERAPY, YOU WILL BE SURPRISED AT WHAT YOU MIGHT FIND OUT ABOUT ONE ANOTHER!

Insert Picture Here

078

FIND A PHOTO BOOTH. YOU KNOW WHAT TO DO. TAKE THE MOST RIDICULOUS PICTURES YOU CAN.

Insert Picture Here

079

GO TO A PSYCHIC TOGETHER. EVEN IF YOU DON'T BELIEVE IN PSYCHICS IT WILL BE INTERESTING TO SEE WHAT THEY SAY.

Insert Picture Here

080

GO ON A DOUBLE DATE. MAKE SURE YOU FIND PEOPLE YOU WILL HAVE A GOOD TIME WITH.

Insert Picture Here

081

GO TO AN OPEN MIC NIGHT. YOU WILL EITHER SEE SOMEONE GREAT OR GET DRUNK ENOUGH TO THINK SOMEONE IS GREAT.

Insert Picture Here

082

HEAD TO A CONVENTION. THIS COULD BE ANY CONVENTION FROM CARS AND TATTOOS TO MUSIC OR COMIC BOOKS.

Insert Picture Here

083

GO TO THE CIRCUS. THERE IS ALWAYS SOMETHING FASCINATING TO WITNESS AT THE CIRCUS.

084

GO TO A SHOPPING CENTRE AND TRY ON MOST RIDICULOUS OUTFITS. YOU CAN EVEN PICK EACH OTHER'S OUTFITS TO TRY ON.

085

RENT A LUXURY OR SPORTS CAR AND DRIVE WHEREVER YOU PLEASE. THIS MIGHT BE A BIT EXPENSIVE BUT YOU WILL FEEL LIKE A MILLIONAIRE.

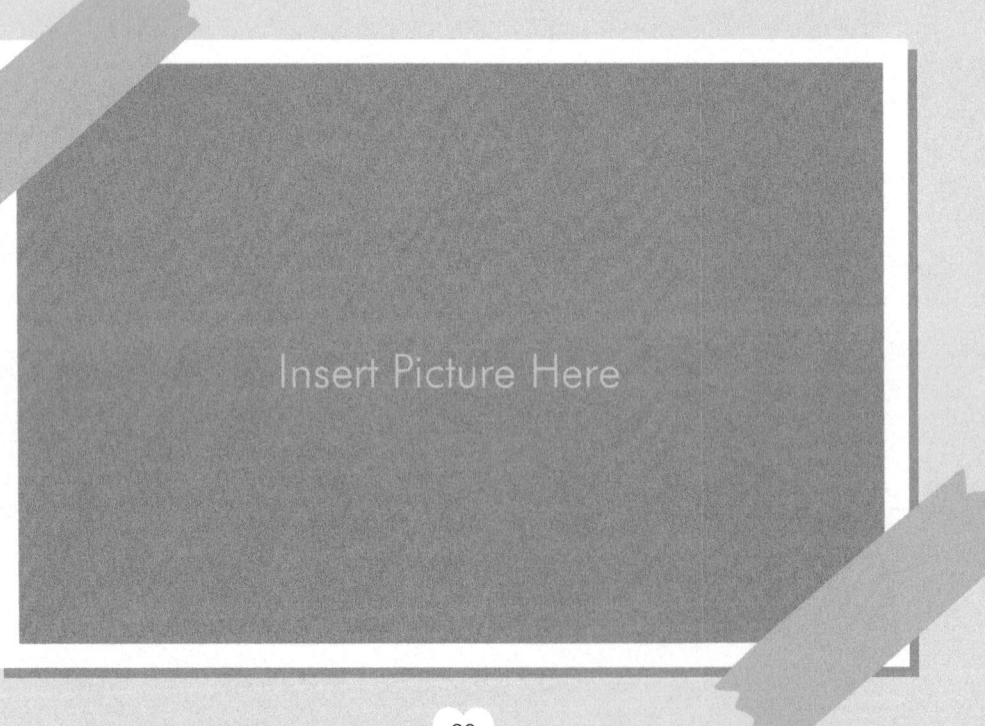

Insert Picture Here

086

PLAY PINBALL. HIGHEST SCORE GETS A MASSAGE FROM THE OTHER PERSON.

087

GO SEE A PROFESSIONAL STAND UP COMEDIAN. BEST PART IS, YOU DON'T HAVE TO GET DRUNK TO LAUGH AT THEIR JOKES.

Insert Picture Here

088

FIND A WORLD RECORD AND ATTEMPT TO BREAK IT. DON'T WORRY, THERE ARE PLENTY OF RECORDS FOR YOU TO CHOOSE FROM.

Insert Picture Here

089

RECREATE YOUR FIRST DATE.

Insert Picture Here

090

FIGURE OUT A BUDGET AND TRY TO PLAN YOUR NEXT VACATION. YOU MAY BE SURPRISED AT THE POSSIBILITIES WITHIN YOUR BUDGET.

Insert Picture Here

091

GO FOR A RIDE ON A CAMEL TOGETHER.

Insert Picture Here

SEASONAL DATES

These are the dates you can complete only at certain times throughout the year

092

CARVE A PUMPKIN TOGETHER.

093

PAINT EASTER EGGS TOGETHER.

Insert Picture Here

094

SET UP YOUR CHRISTMAS TREE.

Insert Picture Here

095

CREATE YOUR OWN UGLY CHRISTMAS SWEATER USING ANY MATERIALS YOU WANT.

Insert Picture Here

096

BUILD A SNOWMAN. IF YOU LIVE IN A PLACE WITH NO SNOW, YOU NEED TO GO ON VACATION.

Insert Picture Here

097

GO SLEDDING. IF YOU LIVE IN A PLACE WITH NO SNOW, YOU CAN ALWAYS GO SLEDDING ON A HILL.

Insert Picture Here

098

BUILD A SANDCASTLE AT THE BEACH. MAKE SURE IT'S HOT OUTSIDE OTHERWISE IT WON'T BE AS FUN.

Insert Picture Here

099

BAKE YOUR OWN CHRISTMAS GINGERBREAD MEN.

Insert Picture Here

100

YOU NEED TO GO ON ANY DATE PARTNER 1 DECIDES TO.

Insert Picture Here

101

YOU NEED TO GO ON ANY DATE PARTNER 2 DECIDES TO GO ON

Insert Picture Here

WIN $300*

❤ **1**   **Scan** the QR code on the bottom right corner.

❤ **2**   **Follow** us on Instagram.

❤ **3**   **Complete** at least 91 of the 101 activities in the book along with the images and send us a message on Instagram.

*All qualified contestants will be placed in a raffle and the winner will be drawn and notified through Instagram on May 1st 2022.

SCAN ME

WE HOPE WE GUIDED YOUR RELATIONSHIP TO THE NEXT LEVEL...

IF YOU WANT TO **HELP OTHER COUPLES** LIKE YOU TAKE THEIR RELATIONSHIP TO THE NEXT STEP...

...CONSIDER LEAVING A QUICK **30–SECOND** REVIEW ON AMAZON.

Golden Lion Publications

Printed in Great Britain
by Amazon